GRAPHIC HISTORY

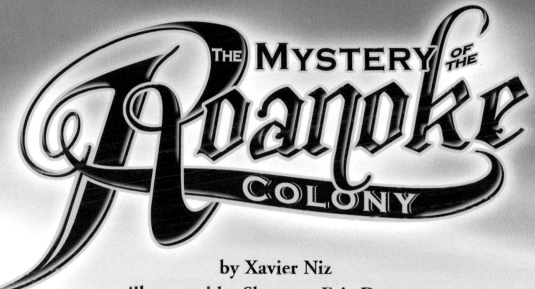

THE MYSTERY OF THE Roanoke COLONY

by Xavier Niz
illustrated by Shannon Eric Denton

Consultant:
Dr. E. Thomson Shields Jr., Director
Roanoke Colonies Research Office
East Carolina University
Greenville, N.C.

Capstone press

Mankato, Minnesota

Graphic Library is published by Capstone Press,
151 Good Counsel Drive, P.O. Box 669, Mankato, Minnesota 56002.
www.capstonepress.com

Printed in the United States of America

1 2 3 4 5 6 11 10 09 08 07 06

Library of Congress Cataloging-in-Publication Data
Niz, Xavier.
The mystery of the Roanoke Colony / by Xavier Niz; illustrated by Shannon Eric Denton.
p. cm.—(Graphic library. Graphic history)
Summary: "In graphic novel format, tells the mysterious story of the disappearance of a group of early American colonists"—Provided by publisher.
Includes bibliographical references and index.
ISBN-13: 978-0-7368-6494-7 (hardcover)
ISBN-10: 0-7368-6494-6 (hardcover)
ISBN-13: 978-0-7368-7530-1 (softcover pbk.)
ISBN-10: 0-7368-7530-1 (softcover pbk.)
1. Roanoke Colony—Juvenile literature. 2. Roanoke Island (N.C.)—History—16th century—Juvenile literature. I. Denton, Shannon Eric. II. Title. III. Series.
F229.N59 2007
975.6'175—dc22 2006007791

Graphic Designers
Jason Knudson and Kim Brown

Colorist
Kristen Fitzner Denton

Editor
Martha E. H. Rustad

Table of Contents

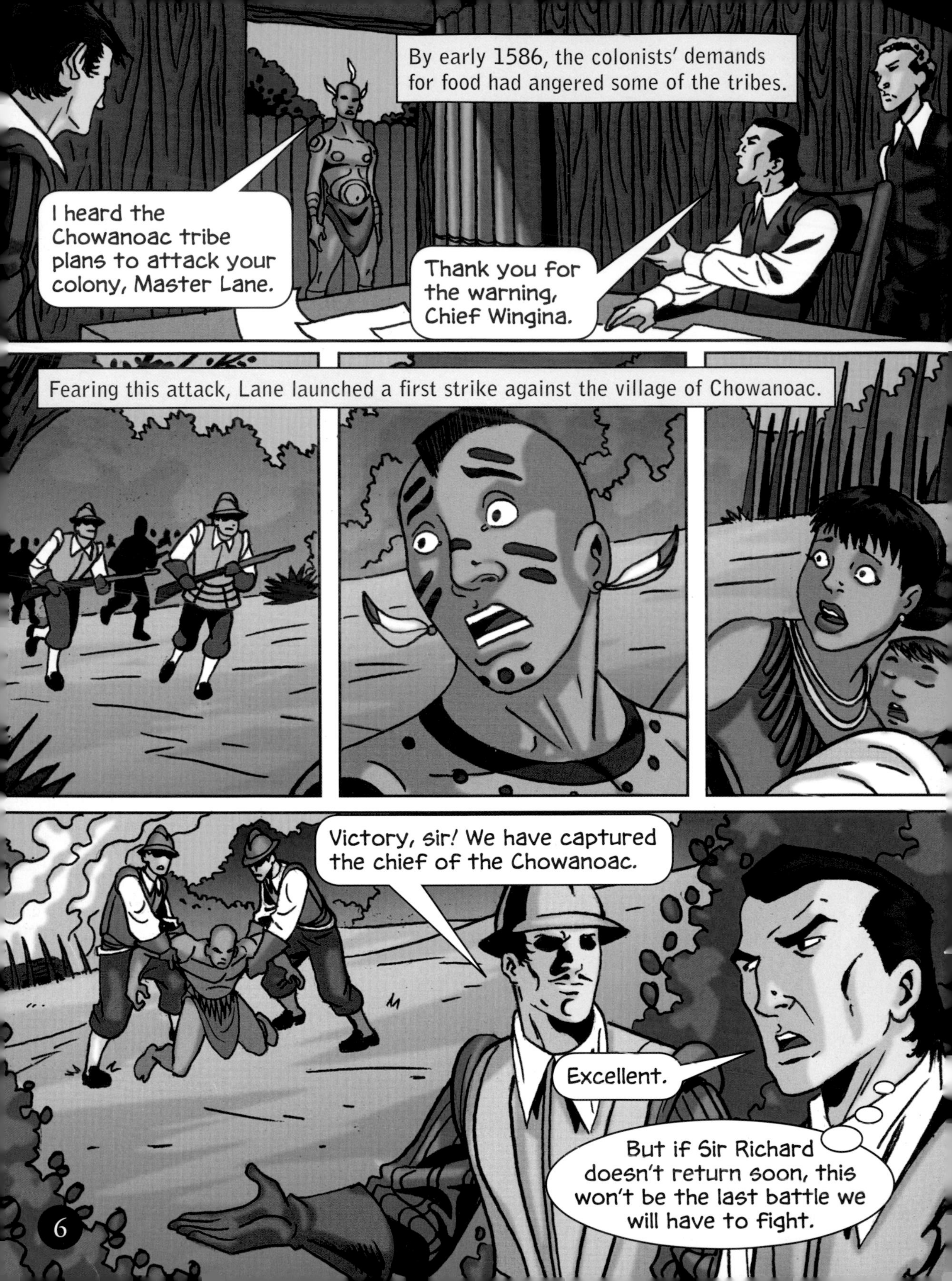
By early 1586, the colonists' demands for food had angered some of the tribes.
I heard the Chowanoac tribe plans to attack your colony, Master Lane.
Thank you for the warning, Chief Wingina.
Fearing this attack, Lane launched a first strike against the village of Chowanoac.
Victory, sir! We have captured the chief of the Chowanoac.
Excellent.
But if Sir Richard doesn't return soon, this won't be the last battle we will have to fight.

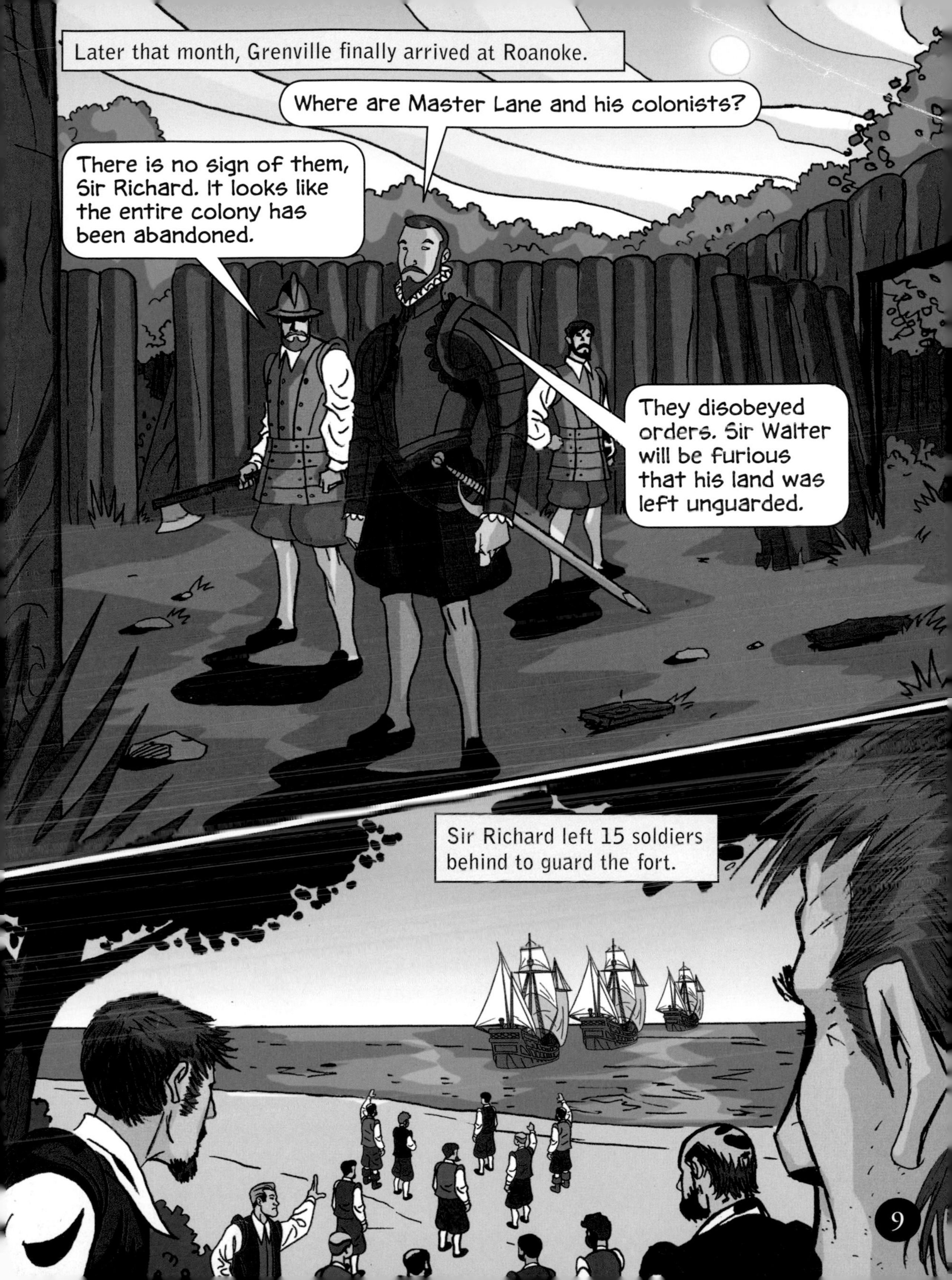

Later that month, Grenville finally arrived at Roanoke.
Where are Master Lane and his colonists?
There is no sign of them, Sir Richard. It looks like the entire colony has been abandoned.
They disobeyed orders. Sir Walter will be furious that his land was left unguarded.
Sir Richard left 15 soldiers behind to guard the fort.

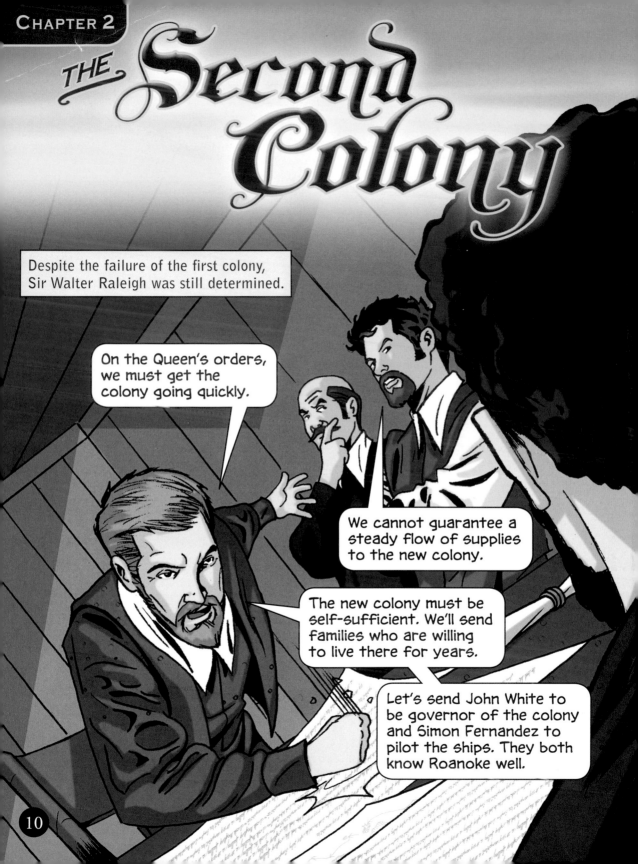

CHAPTER 3

A Colony in Peril

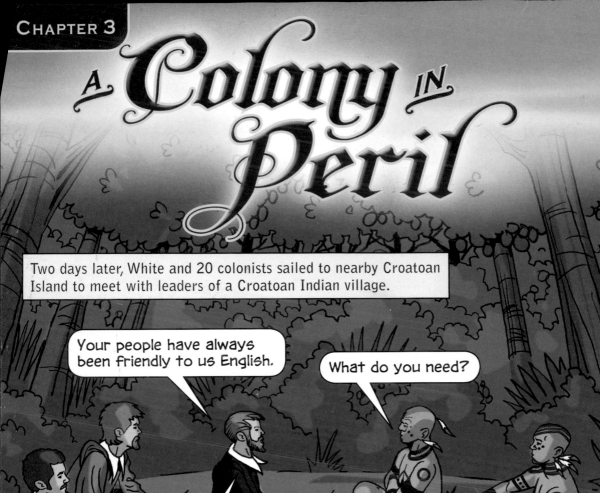

Two days later, White and 20 colonists sailed to nearby Croatoan Island to meet with leaders of a Croatoan Indian village.

Your people have always been friendly to us English.

What do you need?

We cannot find the Englishmen who were left on Roanoke Island more than a year ago.

And one of our men was killed two days ago. Do you know what happened?

Yes. We know what happened to your friends.

Roanoke Island

Croatoan Island

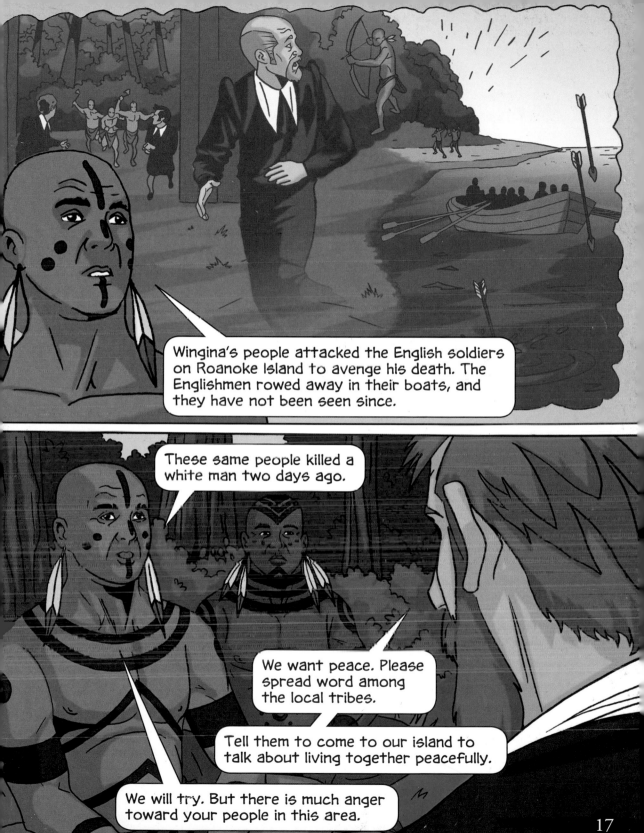

17

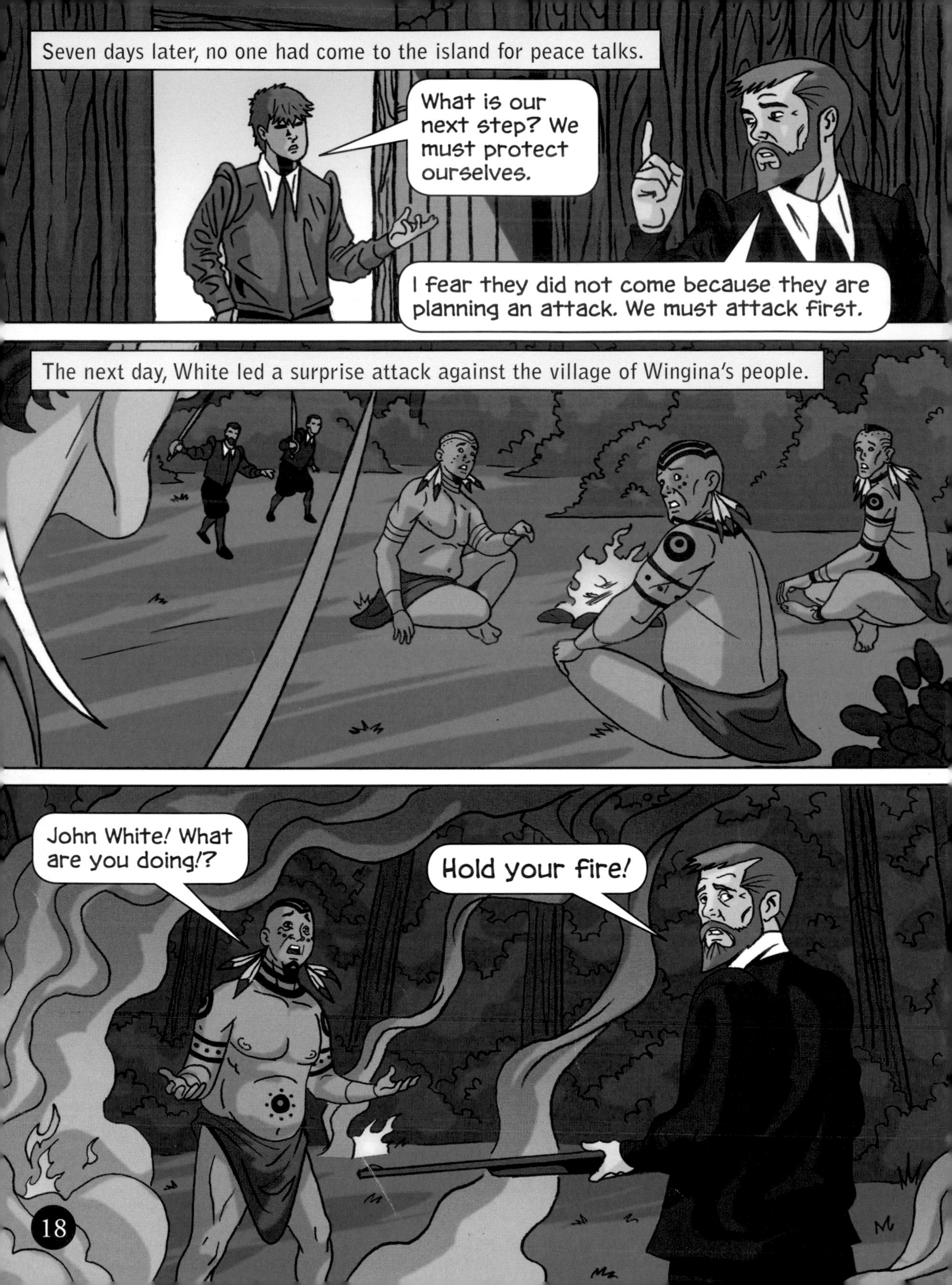
Seven days later, no one had come to the island for peace talks.
What is our next step? We must protect ourselves.
I fear they did not come because they are planning an attack. We must attack first.
The next day, White led a surprise attack against the village of Wingina's people.
John White! What are you doing!?
Hold your fire!

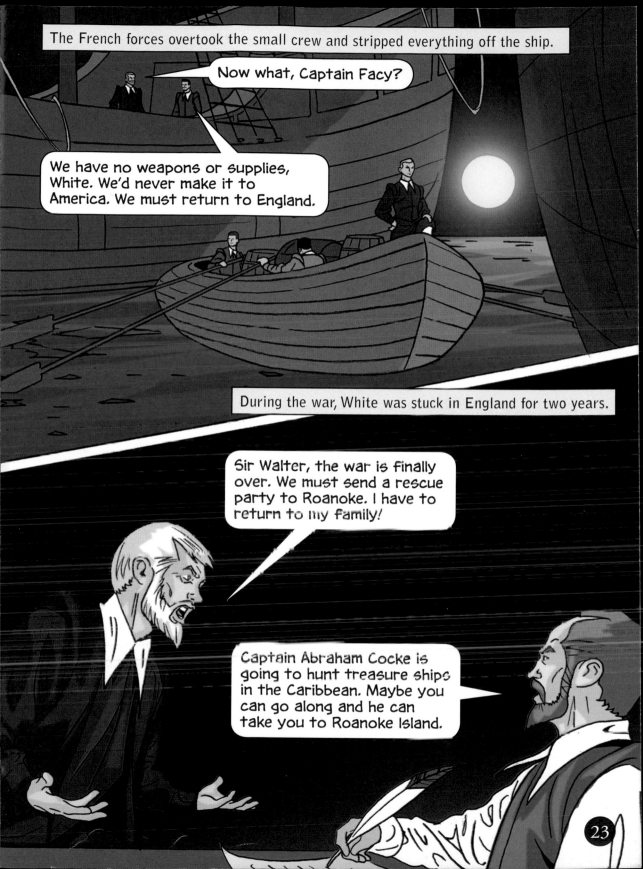

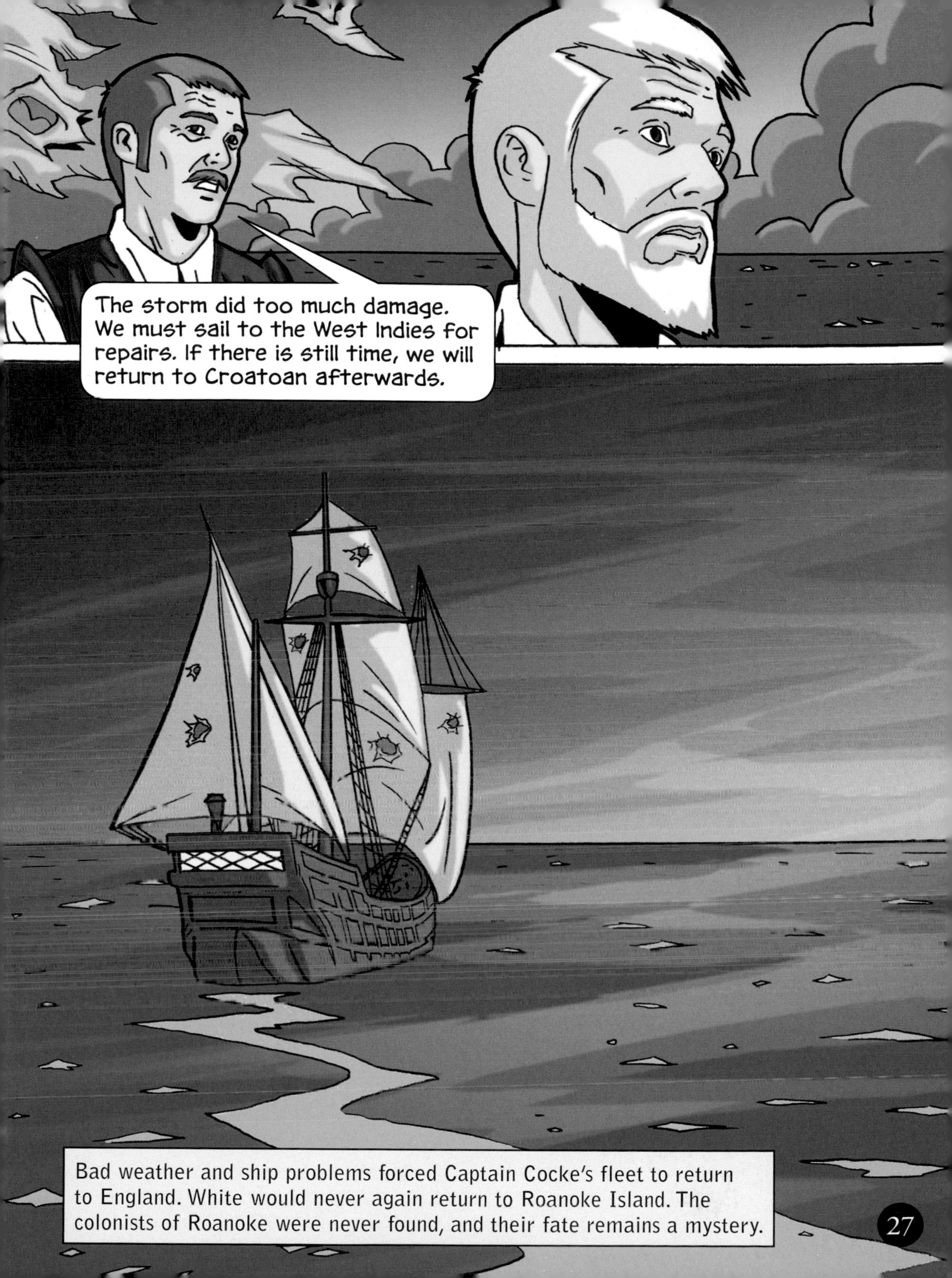
The storm did too much damage. We must sail to the West Indies for repairs. If there is still time, we will return to Croatoan afterwards.
Bad weather and ship problems forced Captain Cocke's fleet to return to England. White would never again return to Roanoke Island. The colonists of Roanoke were never found, and their fate remains a mystery.

More About the Lost Colony

 In 1607, England established a permanent settlement in Jamestown, Virginia. In 1608, the governor of Jamestown, John Smith, spoke to the local Indian Chief Powhatan about the Roanoke colonists. Powhatan confessed that during his war with tribes of Chesapeake Bay, his men attacked and killed a group of Europeans that had settled in the area. As proof he showed Smith a musket barrel and a bronze mortar and certain pieces of iron, which had been theirs.

To add to the mystery, other Europeans likely passed through the Roanoke area. Sailing parties may have stopped in the area as they sailed north out of the Caribbean on their way back to Europe. No one ever saw the Roanoke colonists.

The people of Jamestown continued to search for the lost colonists, sending out two expeditions in 1608. Neither of the groups found any physical evidence of the missing colonists. They did bring back rumors of two white men, four white boys, and a white woman working as slaves in a copper mine run by an Indian leader.

In 1709, surveyor John Lawson reported that the Cape Hatteras and the Croatoan Indians spoke of ancestors who dressed like Europeans and who could read. Lawson also noted that a number of the Croatoans had gray eyes, common in Europeans but rare among Indians.

 Between 1947 and 1950, archaeologists studying Roanoke Island made an unexpected discovery. They found the remains of Lane's fort buried under several layers of dirt. However, they found no evidence of what happened to the missing colonists.

 Today, many historians believe that the colonists left Roanoke Island soon after White's departure and split into two groups. One group went to Croatoan to watch for English ships. A larger group moved north to Chesapeake Bay. There colonists lived alongside a Chesapeake tribe until they were killed by an Indian confederacy under the leadership of Chief Powhatan. This is only a theory, however, and many archaeologists and historians continue to search for the true fate of the lost colony.

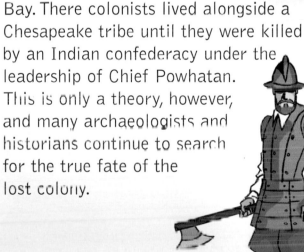

Glossary

abandoned (uh-BAN-duhnd)—deserted or no longer used

assess (uh-SESS)—to judge how good or bad something is

avenge (uh-VENGE)—to get back at someone for hurting you

colony (KOL-uh-nee)—a territory that has been settled by people from another country and is controlled by that country

expedition (ek-spuh-DISH-uhn)—a long journey for a certain purpose, such as exploring

fleet (FLEET)—a group of ships

self-sufficient (SELF suh-FISH-uhnt)—able to take care of one's own needs without help from others

Internet Sites

FactHound offers a safe, fun way to find Internet sites related to this book. All of the sites on FactHound have been researched by our staff.

Here's how:

1. *Visit www.facthound.com*
2. Type in this special code **0736864946** for age-appropriate sites. Or enter a search word related to this book for a more general search.
3. Click on the **Fetch It** button.

FactHound will fetch the best sites for you!

Read More

Dolan, Edward F. *Lost Colony of Roanoke.* New York: Benchmark Books/Marshall Cavendish, 2002.

Fritz, Jean. *The Lost Colony of Roanoke.* New York: G.P. Putnam's Sons, 2004.

Petrie, Kristin. *Sir Walter Raleigh.* Explorers. Edina, Minn.: Abdo, 2006.

Yolen, Jane, and Heidi Elisabet Yolen Stemple. *Roanoke: The Lost Colony: An Unsolved Mystery from History.* New York: Simon & Schuster Books for Young Readers, 2003.

Bibliography

Hakluyt, Richard. *Voyages and Discoveries; The Principal Navigations, Voyages, Traffiques, and Discoveries of the English Nation.* Harmondsworth, England: Penguin, 1972.

Kupperman, Karen Ordahl. *Roanoke, The Abandoned Colony.* Totowa, N.J.: Rowman & Allanheld, 1984.

Miller, Lee. *Roanoke: Solving the Mystery of the Lost Colony.* New York: Arcade, 2001.

Noël Hume, Ivor. *The Virginia Adventure: Roanoke to James Towne: An Archaeological and Historical Odyssey.* Charlottesville: University Press of Virginia, 1997.

Quinn, David B. *Set Fair For Roanoke: Voyages And Colonies, 1584–1606.* Chapel Hill, London: University of North Carolina Press, 1985.

Index